Ben's red

Beverley Randell
Illustrated by Naomi Lewis

Here is my red car.

3

It has wheels

with tires.

It has doors

with handles.

It has windows

with windshield wipers.

It has a steering wheel.

It has lights.

It has a roof-rack

with a bag.

It has a trailer

with a boat.

Look at my red car!